plant
parts

Roots

Melanie Waldron

Raintree

Raintree is an imprint of Capstone Global Library Limited, a company incorporated in England and Wales having its registered office at 7 Pilgrim Street, London, EC4V 6LB – Registered company number: 6695582

www.raintreepublishers.co.uk
myorders@raintreepublishers.co.uk

Text © Capstone Global Library Limited 2014
First published in hardback in 2014
The moral rights of the proprietor have been asserted.

Edited by Sian Smith and Adrian Vigliano
Designed by Cynthia Akiyoshi
Original illustrations © HL Studios
Illustrated by HL Studios
Picture research by Mica Brancic
Originated by Capstone Global Library Ltd
Printed in China by CTPS

ISBN 978 1 406 27479 0
17 16 15 14 13
10 9 8 7 6 5 4 3 2 1

British Library Cataloguing in Publication Data
Waldron, Melanie
Roots (Plant parts)
A full catalogue record for this book is available from the British Library.

Acknowledgements
We would like to thank the following for permission to reproduce photographs: Capstone Publishers pp. 10, 11, 18, 19 (© Karon Dubke); Naturepl.com pp. 4 (© Mark Taylor), 14 (© Juan Manuel Borrero), 22 (© Jose B. Ruiz), 23 (© Jouan & Rius), 25 (© Konrad Wothe), 27 (© Tim Laman), 28 (© Gary K. Smith); Science Photo Library pp. 9 (Steve Gschmeissner), 17 (Dr Jeremy Burgess); Shutterstock pp. 5 (Gyuszko-Photo), 6 (Lauren Hamilton), 7 (Mazzzur), 15 (Fedorov Oleksiy), 20 (Denis and Yulia Pogostins), 21 (dabjola), 26 (Catalin Petolea), 13 bottom (Milos Luzanin), 13 top (Inc), imprint page (© sevenke), title page (© milezaway); SuperStock pp. 24 (Biosphoto), 29 (Stock Connection).

Cover photograph reproduced with permission of Shutterstock (© milezaway).

We would like to thank Michael Bright for his invaluable help in the preparation of this book.

Every effort has been made to contact copyright holders of any material reproduced in this book. Any omissions will be rectified in subsequent printings if notice is given to the publisher.

Contents

Some words are shown in bold, **like this**. You can find out what they mean by looking in the glossary.

Hidden strengths

Look at the plants growing in gardens, parks, forests, and fields near you. They are all held in position by their roots, hidden below the ground. Imagine a huge tree with its branches and even its trunk swaying on a windy day. The tree's roots hold it all in place and stop it from being blown over.

This hawthorn tree has grown in this bent shape because of the windy place it lives in. The roots are strong enough to stop it from toppling over.

Water soaks into the soil and the plant's roots suck it up.

Important roots

Roots can have three important roles. They hold plants in place in the ground. They take in water and **nutrients** from soil for the rest of the plant to use. Some also store food for the plant.

Strong roots

If you grab a big handful of long grass and try to pull it out of the ground, it is almost impossible! The strength of all the roots together makes it too difficult. If you select just one grass stem, it is much easier to pull it out.

5

Working together

Roots are very important parts of plants. They work together with other plant parts to keep the plant healthy and help it to grow.

These plants may look different, but the same basic parts make each plant able to grow and live.

The plant's **stem** rises from the ground, above the roots. It supports the rest of the plant. Tubes inside the stem carry water and food to all the parts of the plant. The plant's leaves use sunlight and a gas from the air called **carbon dioxide** to make food for the plant.

Flowers and seeds

Plants grow flowers to make seeds. Flowers need to get **pollen** from other flowers in order to make seeds. Pollen can be carried between flowers by animals, or by the wind. Once a plant has made seeds, these can set down roots and grow in new places.

Huge plants, tiny flowers

All **deciduous** trees have flowers. Some are quite easy to see, such as on magnolia trees. Others are tiny and hard to spot, such as on ash trees.

These apples have grown from pollinated flowers. The seeds are inside the fruits.

Inside a root

Roots take in water and nutrients through tiny **root hairs** near the ends of smaller roots. Nutrients are chemicals found in the soil. They dissolve into the soil water, and this water can move into the root hairs.

This diagram shows what is inside roots. The tiny root hairs suck in water from the soil.

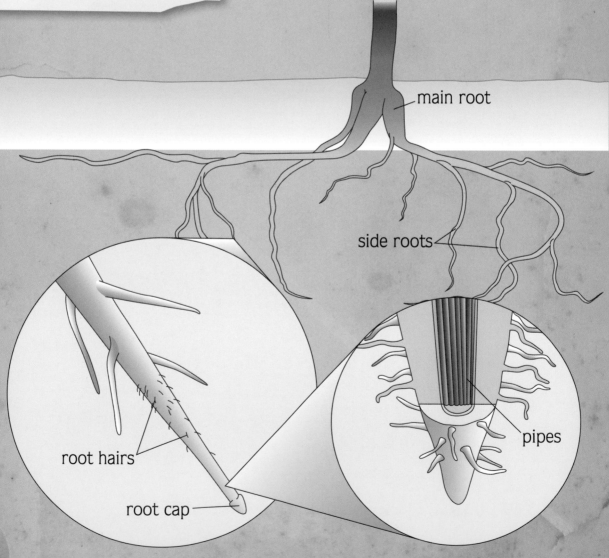

main root

side roots

root hairs

root cap

pipes

Moving water

Once the soil water is inside the tiny root hairs, it can move into the smaller roots. Then it moves through little tubes into the bigger roots. Eventually, it travels up to the stem and to the rest of the plant.

You can see the thin root hairs and the root cap on this magnified poppy plant root.

The water can move upwards because plants lose water through their leaves. Water flows from the stem to replace the water lost in the leaves. Water flows from the roots to replace the water in the stem.

Staying upright

Small plants with soft, bendy stems need water inside them to stay upright. With enough water, the plant is firm and strong. Without water, the plant flops over like a burst balloon. This is called wilting.

Try this!

Try this experiment to see how important roots are to a plant.

You will need:
- two bean seeds
- two small pots
- some soil
- water
- paper
- scissors
- pen

1 Plant two bean seeds in two small pots filled with soil. Make sure there is the same amount of soil in each pot. Give each pot the same amount of water. Put the pots somewhere warm and light, such as a sunny windowsill.

2 After a few weeks, your bean seeds will have grown into little seedlings. Very carefully, remove the seedlings from the soil and lay them down on some paper. Can you see the tiny roots coming from the bottom of each seed?

3 Now cut the tiny roots off one of the seedlings, as close to the seed as possible. Leave the other seedling as it is.

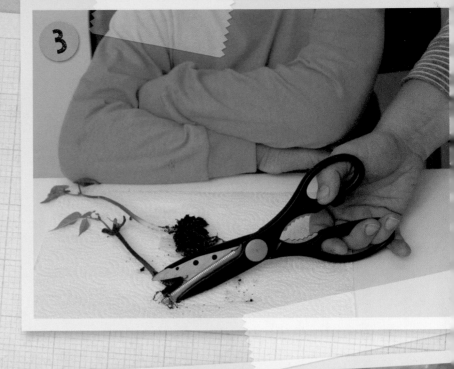

4 Put both seedlings back into their pots, marking the one with cut roots with a cross. Make sure you give each one the same amount of water if they look a bit dry.

5 Now watch how well your seedlings grow over the next few weeks. Has the one with cut roots grown as big or as fast as the other one?

What next?

You could try this experiment using four or five bean seeds. Cut off each one's roots at different times, for example a week apart. Which one grows best?

Different roots

Roots can be different shapes and sizes, depending on the plant they support. Some plants grow one main **tap root**. This grows deep down into the soil, with other smaller side roots branching off it.

This diagram shows a plant with a tap root, and a plant with fibrous roots.

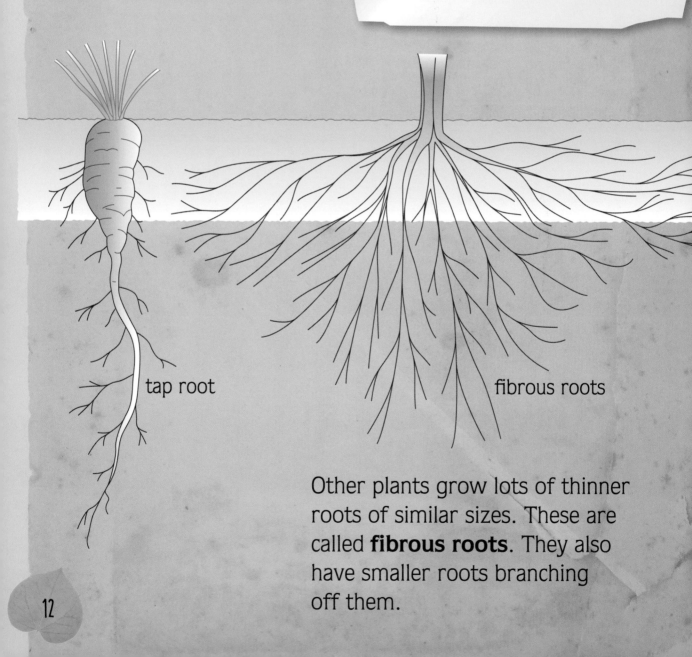

tap root

fibrous roots

Other plants grow lots of thinner roots of similar sizes. These are called **fibrous roots**. They also have smaller roots branching off them.

Storing food

In winter, some plants look like they wither and die. However, many have special roots that store food for the plant over the winter. For example, carrots and beetroot have tap roots that swell up, keeping the plant alive. In the spring, the plant can grow again from the roots.

We eat the swollen tap roots of carrot plants.

Growing around

As roots push their way through the soil, they sometimes come up against rocks and large stones. They can't push through these, so they grow around them. Growing carrots in stony soil will give you some funny-shaped food!

13

Binding the soil

Plant roots do another very important job. They stop the soil they are growing in from being blown or washed away. The **network** of roots binds the soil together and holds it in place. A good example of this is a **sand dune** with grass growing on it. Without the grass roots holding the sand in place, the dune would simply be blown away.

Dunes with grass on them are usually taller than the surrounding area because the sand doesn't get blown away.

The soil below this tree has been blown or washed away. The tree's roots are holding the top layers together to create a ledge at the top.

Spreading wide

Roots don't always go very deep into the soil. Even tree roots don't usually grow more than about 1.5 metres (2 yards) deep into the soil. However, they spread out over a very large area. Often, the roots spread wider than the tree is tall. This means that the roots can hold a large area of soil together.

Animal homes

Animals that live underground, such as rabbits, otters, and badgers, often live in dens among tree roots. The roots stop the dens from collapsing. Roots also help to keep the dens dry, as they suck up water.

New roots

New plants grow from seeds. When a seed has enough water, air, and warmth, it begins to **germinate**. This means that it starts to sprout a tiny root and a tiny **shoot**.

This diagram shows a seed becoming a seedling.

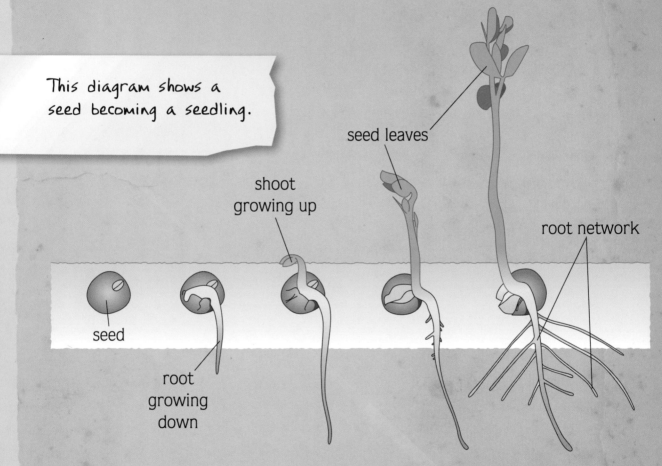

seed leaves

shoot growing up

root network

seed

root growing down

The tiny root pushes through the seed shell and starts to grow down into the ground. The tiny shoot grows upwards to become the plant's stem. The root and the shoot respond to **gravity**. This means that no matter which way up the seed is lying, the root will always grow downwards and the shoot will always grow upwards.

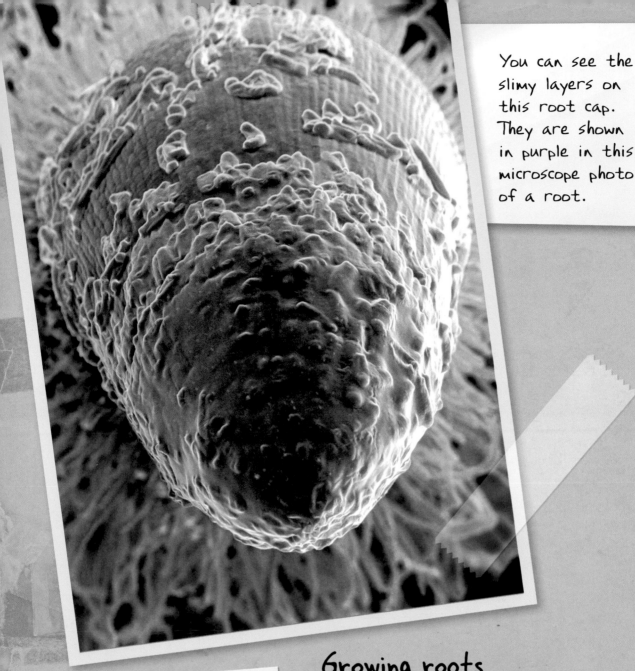

Growing roots

The root is protected by a root cap at its tip. This has slimy layers that can rub off as it pushes into the soil. It protects the rest of the root. The root behind the root cap gets longer and thicker and starts to grow side roots. These also have root caps.

Rock splitting roots

Some roots grow down through cracks in rocks. As they get longer and thicker, they force the rock to split apart. This can cause rocks to tumble down from cliff faces.

Try this!

In this experiment, you will see how gravity affects roots as they grow from a seed.

You will need:

- clear plastic container
- scissors
- newspaper
- cotton wool ball
- bean seed

1 Take a see-through plastic container, such as a small bottle. Carefully cut the top off so you can easily get your hand inside it.

2 Pack the inside of the bottle with some old newspaper. Take a cotton wool ball and place a bean seed onto it. Wet the cotton wool, then carefully slide it down the side of the bottle so that the bean is held between the wet cotton wool and the side of the bottle.

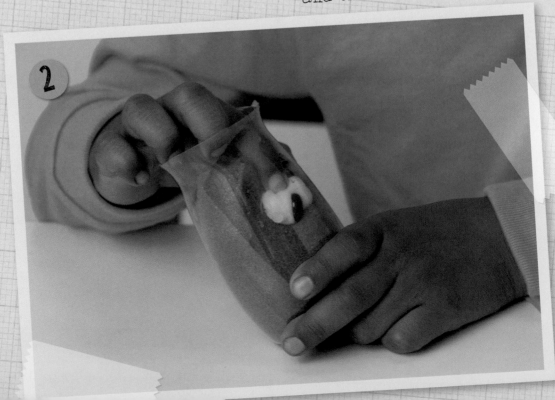

3 Place the bottle somewhere warm, such as a sunny windowsill. Watch it over the next week or so to see if it starts to germinate.

4 Once your seed has started to germinate, you will see its tiny root growing downwards. Now carefully turn your bottle upside down, making sure the bean and cotton wool ball stay in place. The root will now be pointing upwards.

5 Watch your bean over the next week. What does the root do? Does it turn and start growing downwards again?

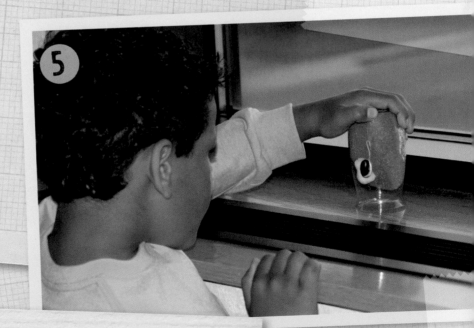

What next?

Try laying the bottle on its side.
What does the root do?

Roots or stems?

Some plant parts growing underground look like they are part of the roots. In fact, they are parts of the stem. **Bulbs** are short, thick underground stem parts. They are surrounded by the bottom ends of leaves, swollen with water and nutrients. **Corms** are similar to bulbs, but are not surrounded by leaf parts. Instead they are swollen stem parts.

Plants that grow bulbs, such as these onion plants, grow roots from the bottom of the bulb.

Tubers and rhizomes

Tubers are parts of the stem that live underground, among the roots. Potatoes are tubers. If you plant them, or leave them in the ground, they will grow into new potato plants.

Rhizomes are underground parts of stems that grow sideways into the soil. New plants can grow upwards from them. Where this happens, new roots grow down from the rhizome into the soil.

Root tubers

Potatoes are stem tubers. Root tubers are similar, but they grow from the roots. Sweet potatoes and yams are root tubers that we eat.

New roots have grown down from this rhizome and new plants have grown upwards.

Growing on others

Not all plants have roots that grow in the ground. Some plants have roots that grow in other plants! These plants grow their roots in the stems of other plants. They take food, water, and nutrients from the plant that they are growing into. For example, mistletoe grows high in trees. The seeds are dropped there by birds. The roots grow into cracks in the tree branches. They take water and food from the tree.

Mistletoe grows its own green leaves to make some food, but most of its food is stolen from the tree it grows in.

Growing on roots

Some plants grow from the roots of other plants. They take water, food, and nutrients from them. Broomrape and toothwort are good examples. They spend most of their time living underground, because they don't need leaves to make their own food. They only stick a stem above ground when they are ready to grow flowers and make seeds.

A strange flower

The rafflesia plant is very strange. It grows in the roots of vines in rainforests. Only its flower is visible. And it is huge! It can be over a metre (3 feet) wide and weigh up to 7 kilograms (15½ pounds).

Visible roots

Not all roots are hidden below the ground. Some plants have roots that grow above ground.

This orchid plant is an epiphyte.

Epiphytes are plants that live high up on other plants. This helps them to get more light to make food. They don't take water and food from the plants they grow on. Their roots wind around the plant for support. Orchid roots can take in water from the air, and bromeliad plants catch rainfall in their leaves.

Reaching the ground

Strangler fig plants grow high on trees. Their roots grow downwards until they reach the ground. Then they grow into the ground. Eventually, strangler figs grow so large that they cover and kill the tree they started growing on.

The roots of this strangler fig are reaching down towards the soil.

Roots into walls

Ivy is a climbing plant. You can see it growing up trees and buildings. It sprouts little roots all the way up its stem. These roots grow onto the tree or building, supporting the ivy as it grows upwards.

Banyan trees grow **aerial roots** down from their branches to the ground. These thicken and eventually become the trunks of new trees.

Roots around the world

Plants can grow in all sorts of places around the world. Many have special **adaptations** to help them grow in difficult places. Some have root adaptations.

In desert areas, cactus plants grow very long roots, but they grow very **shallow** along the ground. This helps them to take advantage of any rainfall. Some desert plants have thickened roots where they can store water.

Plants, such as moss, can grow on bare rock. They attach themselves to the rock surface and absorb water through their leaves.

These strange pointed roots are growing upwards out of the water to get oxygen.

Rivers, ponds, and coasts

Some plants growing in water have their roots in the mud at the bottom. Other roots dangle free in the water. Large plants such as mangroves have **prop roots** that grow from the stem, down into the water.

On stony beaches, plants have long, sprawling roots. This helps them stay rooted in the stones, and means they can reach deep water.

Growing upwards

Trees such as mangroves and swamp cypresses that live in wet areas need breathing roots. These are special roots to help them get oxygen from the air. They grow upwards from the main roots in the ground.

Roots and us

We eat lots of different kinds of roots. Carrots, radishes, parsnips, turnips, beetroot, sweet potatoes, yams, and cassava are all roots that we eat.

Parsnips are sweet and creamy. Many years ago, before sugar was easy to get hold of, people used parsnips to sweeten foods such as cakes. The orange colour in carrots is a chemical that can help protect against diseases such as cancer.

Many plant roots are colourful and delicious!

28

These tree roots are pushing up the pavement!

Troublesome roots

Sometimes large roots, especially tree roots, can cause us problems. They are strong enough to lift paving stones and crack wall foundations. In some soils, large roots can suck lots of water out in the summer. This causes the ground to shrink. Then in the winter the ground gets wet again and swells. This shrinking and swelling can cause big cracks in buildings.

Orange carrots?

Carrots today are usually orange. When people first grew them, they were mostly purple, white, and yellow. Over the years, farmers carefully chose which plants to make seeds from. Gradually, the colour of most carrots became more and more orange. You can sometimes find other colours of carrot at farmers' markets.

29

Glossary

adaptation feature of a living thing that has changed over time to suit the environment

aerial root root that grows above the ground. Some aerial roots reach right down to the ground while others never reach the ground.

bulb part of a plant's stem that stays underground, is surrounded by fleshy leaves, and can produce new plants

carbon dioxide gas with no colour or smell that is found in the air

corm fleshy part of a plant's stem that stays underground and can produce new plants

deciduous plants, such as trees, that lose their leaves every year

epiphyte plant that grows on another plant but doesn't take water or nutrients from it

fibrous root thin root that grows down from a plant along with lots of other fibrous roots

germinate start to grow into a new plant

gravity force that pulls things down towards the surface of Earth

network system of things that are linked together

nutrient chemical that helps plants to live and grow

pollen fine powder made in plant flowers. It is used by plants to fertilize flowers to make seeds.

pollinated when pollen, made by the male part of a flower, lands on the female parts of a flower. A pollinated flower can then make seeds.

prop root root that grows out and down from the stem, reaching the ground and providing support for the plant

rhizome stem part that grows sideways underground and can produce new plants

root cap tough cap that covers the ends of roots and protects them as they push through the soil

root hair thin, hair-like strand that grows from a root and can absorb water and nutrients from the soil

sand dune large mound of sand that is built up by the wind and often held together by plant roots

shallow not deep

shoot new growth on a plant, and also the first bit of a plant to grow from a germinated seed

stem main part of a plant that supports the branches, leaves, and flowers

tap root large main root of a plant that usually grows straight down. Smaller roots branch off from the tap root.

tuber short, thick, roundish stem parts that grow underground and can produce new plants

Find out more

Books

Growing Plants: Leaves, Roots, and Shoots, Jim Pipe (Franklin Watts, 2008)

Plants (Wildlife Watchers), Terry Jennings (QED, 2010)

Roots (Plants), Patricia Whitehouse (Raintree, 2009)

Zoom! The Invisible World of Plants, Camilla de la Bedoyere (QED, 2012)

Websites

www.bbc.co.uk/nature/plants This website has lots of information about plants. There are also some amazing film clips of plants all around the world.

www.bgfl.org/bgfl/custom/resources_ftp/client_ftp/ks2/science/s_plants/index.htm Have a look at this website to find out more about how plants work.

www.rhs.org.uk/Children/For-kids/Mostest-plants Go to this web page to find out interesting facts about the tallest tree, smelliest flower, and speediest seed!

Places to visit

The Natural History Museum in London has hundreds of displays and activities. You can learn about how plants and animals have changed over time, and how scientists work to discover all about the natural world.

The Royal Botanic Gardens in Kew in London has plants from all over the world.

The Eden Project in Cornwall is a series of huge domed greenhouses, one of which contains a rainforest! There are fun activities and amazing things to learn about plants.

Go for a walk in your local nature park! Spend time looking closely at all the different roots you can see.

Index